www.booksbyboxer.com

Published by
Books By Boxer, Leeds, LS13 4BS UK
Books by Boxer (EU), Dublin D02 P593 IRELAND
© Books By Boxer 2021
All Rights Reserved
MADE IN MALTA

ISBN: 9781909732865

THE FIRST EVER BICYCLES WERE MADE ALMOST ENTIRELY OF WOOD, AND SEVERAL THOUSAND WERE BUILT AND USED. UNSURPRISINGLY, ACCIDENTS WERE SO FREQUENT THAT THE BRITISH POLICE PROHIBITED THEIR USE!

Recent advances in technology mean that wooden bicycles are safer and much more durable than what they were in the 1800's. In 2008, Phil Bridge created a prototype of a cardboard bicycle.

PRODUCED BY THE COMPANY
SANTOS AND THE UNIVERISTY OF
SOUTH AUSTRALIA IN 2015,
THE WORLD'S LONGEST TANDEM
BIKE IS A WHOPPING 20 METERS
LONG AND SEATS
35 PEOPLE.

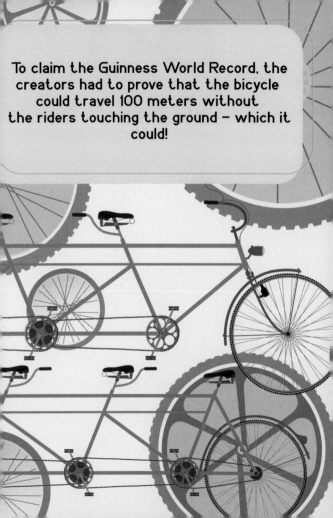

To claim the Guinness World Record, the creators had to prove that the bicycle could travel 100 meters without the riders touching the ground – which it could!

A BICYCLE CAN STAY UPRIGHT
WITHOUT A RIDER AS LONG AS IT
IS TRAVELLING 8MPH OR FASTER.
THIS IS DUE TO CERTAIN FACTORS
SUCH AS THE WEIGHT OF THE BIKE
THE ANGLE OF THE BIKE'S FORKS
AND THE CONDITION OF
THE ROAD.

Some celebrities such as Pippa Middleton, Jennifer Lopez, Zac Efron, and even George Clooney enjoy cycling in their free time just as much as the general public!

THE LARGEST RIDEABLE BIKE HAS A WHEEL DIAMETER OF 3.3 METER AND WAS BUILT BY DIDI SENFT FROM GERMANY. ALTHOUGH NOT AS COMMON NOW, LARGE BICYCL WHEELS WERE THE NORM IN THE 1880S WITH THE AVERAGE FRONT WHEEL SIZE BEING 1.3 METERS.

THIS IS DUE TO THE LACK OF DRIVETRAIN SYSTEMS, MEANING THAT THE ONLY WAY TO PROPEL THE BICYCLE WAS BY DIRECT CRANKING OF THE FRONT WHEEL – THE LARGER THE WHEELS, THE GREATER THE DISTANCE TRAVELLED PER PEDAL STROKE!

Due to the high center-of-gravity and consequent lack of stability, obstacles would often send riders flying face down into the dirt, which created a set of injurious pet names such as a cropper, imperial crowner and the infamous header.

CYCLING IS ON AVERAGE 3 TIMES FASTER THAN WALKING. THE AVERAGE WALKING SPEED IS JUST 3 TO 4 MILES PER HOUR COMPARED TO 10 TO 12 MILES PER HOUR ON A BIKE. IT ALSO EXPENDS ROUGHLY THE SAME AMOUNT OF ENERGY, WHAT AN EFFICIENT WAY TO TRAVEL!

The fastest bicycle speed recorded
is the eye-watering 183.9mph achieved
in 2018 by American cyclist
Denise Mueller-Korenek.

Born into a daredevil sporting family,
she has a cyclist father and midget
derby car racer mother.

Denise Mueller-Korenek

YOU CAN FIT AROUND 15 BIKES IN THE SAME SPACE A SINGLE CAR OCCUPIES. AN AVERAGE CAR IS APROXIMATELY 4.70 METERS LONG AND 1.90 METERS WIDE.

Cycling has a carbon footprint of about 21g of CO_2 per kilometre. That is less than walking or getting the bus and less than a tenth the emissions of driving.

OVER 100 MILLION BICYCLES ARE MANUFACTURED IN THE WORLD EACH YEAR. IT IS ESTIMATED THAT MANUFACTURERS ACROSS THE WORLD PRODUCE 364,000 BICYCLES EVERY SINGLE DAY – THAT'S FOUR BICYCLES EVERY SECOND! THE RESULT IS A GLOBAL INDUSTRY WORTH A HUGE £36BN ($45BN)

THERE ARE TWICE AS MANY
BICYCLES IN THE WORLD
THAN THERE ARE CARS,
THOUGH THE TOTAL AMOUNT
OF CARS TAKE UP MORE SPACE
THAN THE FULL AMOUNT
OF BIKES IN THE WORLD.

The Danish capital, Copenhagen, is considered the most bicycle-friendly city in the world. 52% of the population commutes by bike there!

5% OF ALL TRIPS IN THE UK ARE
MADE WITH A BICYCLE.
THIS IS HIGHER THAN THE USA,
IN WHICH ONLY 1% OF TRIPS ARE
MADE VIA BICYCLE.

The British public spend more than £1.4 billion every year on cycling!

THE UK IS HOME TO OVER 20 MILLION CYCLES, THOUGH CYCLING ONLY MAKES UP FOR 1% OF ROAD TRAFFIC IN GREAT BRITAIN.

World Bicycle Day is on the 3rd June and celebrates all things cycling!

THE FAMOUS WRIGHT BROTHERS OWNED THEIR OWN BIKE REPAIR SHOP WHICH THEY USED DURING THE INVENTION OF THE WORLD'S VERY FIRST SUCCESSFUL AIRPLANE.

They used their bicycle workshop to build the 1903 Wright Flyer!

Depending on the stage of the event, cyclists competing in the Tour De France consume between 5,000 and 7,000 calories a day! This is because they must eat more calories than they burn during each stage of the race.

The professional cyclists burn a combined estimated total of 25 million calories across the three weeks while competing in the Tour De France.

PROFESSIONAL CYCLISTS OFTEN SHAVE THEIR LEGS IN CASE OF INJURIES SUCH AS ROAD RASH, AS SHAVED LEGS MAKE IT EASIER TO CLEAN WOUNDS AND HAVE LESS CHANCE OF DEVELOPING AN INFECTION.

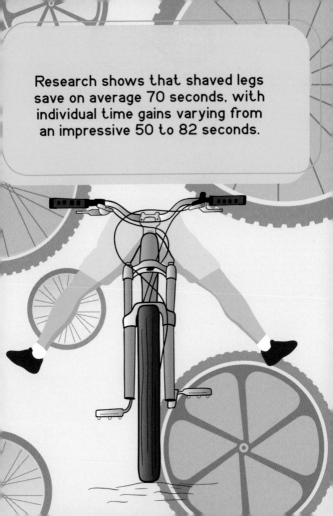

Research shows that shaved legs save on average 70 seconds, with individual time gains varying from an impressive 50 to 82 seconds.

THE WORLD'S FIRST AIR-FILLED
TIRE WAS INVENTED FOR BICYCLES
IN THE LATE 1880S, BUT WASN'T
USED IN THE DEVELOPMENT OF
CARS UNTIL ALMOST 10 YEARS AFTE

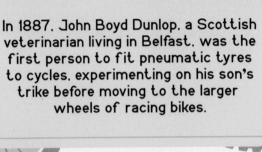

In 1887, John Boyd Dunlop, a Scottish veterinarian living in Belfast, was the first person to fit pneumatic tyres to cycles, experimenting on his son's trike before moving to the larger wheels of racing bikes.

FAMOUS ACTRESS JENNIFER ANISTON WAS ONCE A BIKE MESSENGER IN NEW YORK CITY BEFORE MAKING IT BIG IN HOLLYWOOD, AND SAID IT WAS THE HARDEST JOB SHE'S EVER HAD.

The bike-based, food delivery company Deliveroo have over 3,500 bike couriers in the UK alone!

THE TERM 'BICYCLE' WAS NOT INTRODUCED UNTIL THE 1860s, WHEN THE WORD 'BICYCLETTE' WAS USED IN FRANCE TO DESCRIBE A NEW KIND OF VEHICLE.

In the nineteenth century, Reverend William Barnes – a keen linguist – was one of many who wanted to cleanse the English language of French words. To this end, he proposed that the bicycle be referred to as the "wheelsaddle". Thankfully this didn't catch on.

BEFORE THE WORD 'BICYCLE' BECAME POPULAR, BIKES WERE TYPICALLY CALLED 'VELOCIPEDES'.

Bicycles have had many names throughout history. The Hobby Horse, Dandy Horse, Draisine, Boneshaker and Penny Farthing are just a few other terms bicycles were known as.

THE PENNY-FARTHING IS AN EARLY MODEL OF BIKE WHICH HAD A LARGE FRONT WHEEL AND A SMALL REAR WHEEL. IT'S NAME COMES FROM OLD BRITISH CURRENCY WHERE THE PENNY COIN WAS MUCH LARGER THAN THE FARTHING COIN.

The front wheel of the infamous penny-farthing averaged 130cm and the bicycle commonly weighed up to 22kg!

Penny-farthing bicycle.

SEVEN OUT OF EIGHT
DUTCH PEOPLE OVER THE AGE O
15 HAVE A BICYCLE, AND A MASSIV
30% OF ALL TRIPS IN THE
NETHERLANDS ARE MADE ON
BICYCLE.

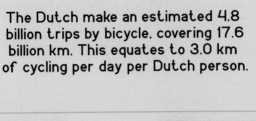

The Dutch make an estimated 4.8 billion trips by bicycle, covering 17.6 billion km. This equates to 3.0 km of cycling per day per Dutch person.

If the number of cyclists were tripled, the rate of motorist–cyclist accidents would be cut in half.

Around 83% of people aged 18 or over who cycle often also own a driving license.

HELMETS HAVE BEEN FOUND TO BE 85% EFFECTIVE IN PREVENTING A HEAD INJURY WHILE CYCLING. HOWEVER, THERE IS NO BRITISH LAW THAT STATES A CYCLIST MUST WEAR A HELMET.

Surprisingly, modern bicycle helmets only became mainstream in 1975 when the company Bell Sports created the modification of motorsports helmets, made of polystyrene foam with a hard Lexan shell.

THE FIRST EVER PROFESSIONAL BIK
RACE TOOK PLACE OUTSIDE OF
PARIS ON MAY 31ST, 1868! THE
RACE WAS 1,200 METRES AND
WAS WON BY EXPATRIATE
ENGLISHMAN JAMES MOORE,
WHO RODE A BICYCLE
WITH SOLID RUBBER
TYRES.

James Moore
Born: 14th January 1849.
Place of Birth: Long Brackland, UK.
Died: 17th July 1935 (aged 86).
Honors include winning the first ever
cycle race (St Cloud, 1868) and the
first ever road race (Paris-Rouven, 1869)

MANY FEMALE-TARGETED BIKES
FROM THE VICTORIAN ERA
THROUGH TO CURRENT TIMES
DON'T HAVE HORIZONTAL
CROSSBARS ON THE FRAMES
DUE TO WOMEN COMMONLY
WEARING DRESSES. THESE BARS
WERE REMOVED IN AN AIM TO
SAVE A WOMEN'S MODESTY
WHEN SHE MOUNTS OR
DISMOUNTS HER BICYCLE.

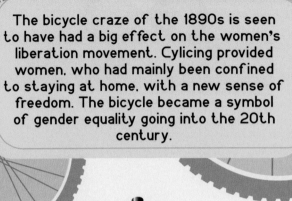

The bicycle craze of the 1890s is seen to have had a big effect on the women's liberation movement. Cylicing provided women, who had mainly been confined to staying at home, with a new sense of freedom. The bicycle became a symbol of gender equality going into the 20th century.

AT ST. HELEN'S SCHOOL IN
NEWBURY, OHIO, UNICYCLING IS
A MANDATORY SUBJECT THAT
MUST BE TAUGHT TO ALL STUDENT
THE ST. HELEN UNICYCLE DRILL TEA
INCLUDES MEMBERS FROM YOUNG
CHILDREN TO GRANDPARENTS
WHO SHARE A LOVE OF
RIDING THIS UNIQUE
PERSONAL TRANSPORTER...

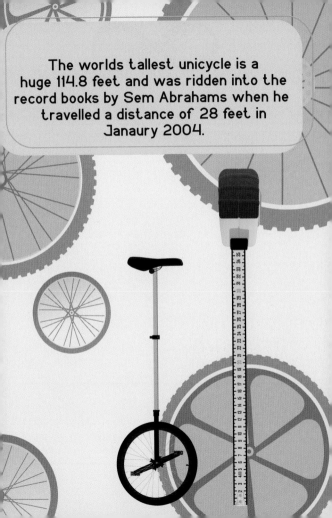

The worlds tallest unicycle is a huge 114.8 feet and was ridden into the record books by Sem Abrahams when he travelled a distance of 28 feet in Janaury 2004.

FLAT ROADS BECAME POPULAR
BECAUSE OF BICYCLES. CARS
COULD GO OVER COBBLESTONE
FAIRLY WELL, BUT BIKES STRUGGLE
THE LOBBYING FOR ROAD
IMPROVEMENT WAS CARRIED OUT
- AND PAID FOR - BY CYCLING
ORGANISATIONS IN THE 1930'S.

Bicycle lanes were first invented in 1890's. These lanes were smoother to ride on compared to cobblestone roads, and helped cyclists stay clear from other vehicles and pedestrians.

HANS AND MARGRET REY FLED
PARIS IN 1940 ON BICYCLES
THAT HANS HAD BUILT.
WITH ONLY A FEW POSESSIONS
ON THEM, ONE OF THE MOST
VALUABLE WAS AN ILLUSTRATED
MANUSCRIPT OF CURIOUS GEORG
WHICH THEY LATER HAD
PUBLISHED IN NEW YORK.

Today, there are over 25 million copies of the original Curious George titles in print. It could be argued that George's first adventure was escaping the Nazi's on a bicycle!

ON 28TH JANUARY, 1896, WALTER ARNOLD FROM EAST PECKHAM, KENT, BECAME THE FIRST PERSON IN GREAT BRITAIN TO BE CHARGED WITH SPEEDING AFTER TRAVELLING A TERRYFING 8MPH - WHICH WAS FOUR TIMES OVER THE LEGAL LIMIT OF 2MPH. THE MOST HILARIOUS PART IS THAT THE POLICEMAN WHICH FINED WALTER EASILY CAUGHT UP WITH HIM ON HIS BICYCLE!

Walter Arnold was charged for four things: using a horseless locomotive on a public road, operating the locomotive with less than three people, travelling more than 2mph, and not clearly displaying his name and address on the locomotive. Walter was found guilty of all four offences and was fined 4 pound and 7 shillings (£260 in our current currency).

IN 1913, THE TOUR DE FRANCE
RULES FORBADE OUTSIDE ASSISTAN
ON BROKEN BICYCLES. ONE RIDER
(WHO HAD TAKEN THE LEAD
AT THE TIME) TREKKED 10 KM
TO A FORGE TO REPAIR THE
BIKE HIMSELF, AFTER HIS FRONT
FORK BROKE. THE CYCLIST, WHO
WAS ALSO A SKILLED MECHANIC,
HAD A CHILD HELP HIM WORK TH
BELLOWS, AND WAS PENALIZED 10
MINUTES DUE TO THIS BREACH
OF RULES.

A cyclist who crashed during the US race
– The Tour of the Gila –
after a dog ran out onto the road,
managed to complete the stage after
borrowing a 1980s mountain bike
from a spectator to ride the final
four kilometres.

During World War Two, the Japanese invaded most of Malaysia while riding on bicycles. Occupying Singapore was Japan's objectiv so members of the Japanese military stole bicycles which were originally imported from Japan.

Since rubber was scarce during the war, once their tires wore out, they rode on their rims and continued their conquest. With the quietness, speed and element of surprise on their side, the Japanese were able to outrun many British soldiers.

IN 1907 THE DELIVERY COMPANY UPS WAS FOUNDED BY TWO TEENAGERS, ONE BICYCLE AND $100 (WHICH WAS BORROWED FROM A FRIEND). JAMES CASEY (19) AND CLAUDE RYAN (18) FOUNDED THE COMPANY IN THE BASEMENT OF A HOTEL IN SEATTLE, AND NOW EMPLOYS PEOPLE IN 220 COUNTRIES ACROSS THE GLOBE!

Almost immediately after the development of the pedal-driven velocipede in the 1860s, people began to use the bicycle for delivery purposes. By the 1870s, the Paris Stock Exchange were frequently hiring bike couriers.

IN 1954, AFTER TELLING HIS PARENTS HE WAS GOING TO SCHOOL, A FIFTEEN YEAR OLD RODE HIS BIKE 700 MILES IN A SINGLE WEEK FROM D.C. TO ATLANTA WITH HIS REASONING BEING THAT HE FELT "HOMESICK FOR DIXIE AND HIS GRANDMOTHER'S FRIED CHICKEN.

The world record for the longest distance of non-stop cycling was achieved by Jai Bhagwan from India in 2018 when he covered 202.1 km in 10 hours, 44 minutes and 5 seconds.

WITH THE HIGHEST BIKE DENSITY IN THE WORLD, THERE ARE MORE BIKES THAN PEOPLE IN THE NETHERLANDS.

THE SMALLEST 'RIDEABLE' BMX WA
INVENTED BY A MAN CALLED BOB
AND HIS FATHER. THE BIKE
MEASURED 19.69 CM TALL AND 7.6
CM FROM WHEEL TO WHEEL.
IT IS SAID THAT THE PEDALS ARE
JUST WIDE ENOUGH TO FIT TWO
TOES AND THE WHEELS ON
THE BIKE ARE THE SIZE OF
ONE SILVER US DOLLAR!

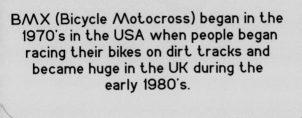

BMX (Bicycle Motocross) began in the 1970's in the USA when people began racing their bikes on dirt tracks and became huge in the UK during the early 1980's.

BICYCLES WERE OFTEN REFERED
TO AS 'BONESHAKERS' BEFORE THE
INVENTION OF INFLATABLE TIRES
DUE TO HOW UNCOMFORTABLE
AND BUMPY THE RIDE COULD GET.
THE "BONESHAKER" WEIGHED 80KG
WHEN IT APPEARED FOR SALE IN
1868 IN PARIS.

When Antonin Magne won the 1934 Tour de France on Mavic aluminum wheel rims, the technology was still illegal, and they were painted to resemble wood.

THE WORD 'BIKE' IN TURKEY IS A FEMALE FIRST NAME WITH THE MEANING QUEEN AND WOMAN! CYCLING IS BECOMING INCREASINGLY POPULAR IN TURKEY WITH THE NUMBER OF BIKES EXPECTED TO SURPASS CARS BY 2023.

Turkey is one of the most popular destinations in the world for cross country cycling!

ON 12 JUNE 1817, A CROWD
GATHERED ALONG THE BEST ROAD
IN MANNHEIM, GERMANY TO
WATCH BARON KARL VON
DRAIS DEMONSTRATE HIS
NEWEST INVENTION, THE
'DRAISIENNE': A TWO-WHEELED,
HORSELESS VEHICLE PROPELLED
BY IT'S RIDER. THIS INVENTION IS
HAILED FOR INSPIRING THE
CREATION OF THE MODERN-DAY
BICYCLE.

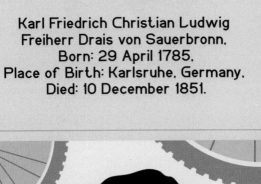

Karl Friedrich Christian Ludwig
Freiherr Drais von Sauerbronn,
Born: 29 April 1785,
Place of Birth: Karlsruhe, Germany,
Died: 10 December 1851.

FOUR BICYCLES ARE PRODUCED EVERY SECOND, WHICH MEANS 345,600 BICYCLES ARE MADE EVERY 24 HOURS!

The largest bicycle manufacturer in the world is Giant Manufacturing Co. Ltd. (Giant Bicycles). Established in 1972 and originating in Taiwan, this company has factories in Taiwan, China, Hungary and the Netherlands.

FRED A. BIRCHMORE, AGED 25 AT THE TIME, CIRCLED THE GLOBE BY BICYCLE IN 1935, WEARING OUT SEVEN SETS OF TIRES ON HIS TRAVELS. HE PEDALED FOR 25,000 MILES AND TRAVELED THE OTHER 15,000 MILES BY BOAT

Fred A. Birchmore
Born: 29th November 1911
Died: 15th April 2012 (Aged 100)
Fred had many hobbies and careers including being a lawyer, professor, author, lecturer, boxer, acrobat, sailor, naval officer in WWII, boxing and sports coach, aviator, archaeologist, ornithologist, scout leader, singer, and farmer.

ONE BIKE IS PURCHASED EVERY TWO SECONDS AROUND THE GLOBE.

The average household spend on bicycles per week amounts up to £1. That s a whole £58.50 less than the total avereage weekly amount for a car per household.

THE FAMOUS CYCLING RACE, THE TOUR DE FRANCE, WAS ESTABLISHED IN 1903. THE EIGHT FASTEST CYCLISTS RECEIVED BETWEEN 50 AND 1,500 FRANCS IN PRIZE MONEY. THE BEST RIDER RECEIVED 3,000 FRANCS AND ALL OTHER CYCLISTS EARNED 95 FRANCS EACH

The longest tour in history took place in 1926 with the route totalling 3,570 miles. The bicycle race was won by Belgian cyclist Lucien Buysse.

BICYCLE THEFT IS THE MOST COMMON CRIME IN AMSTERDAM, WITH NEARLY 10,000 BIKES REPORTED AS STOLEN PER YEAR.

Current estimates suggest that there are approximately 881,000 bikes in Amsterdam, compared to around 851,573 permanent residents.

Frenchman De Sivrac built the first bicycle-type vehicle in 1790, though pedals were added to the invention in 1839 by Scottsman Kirkpatrick Macmillan, who is credited with inventing the real bicycle.

Kirkpatrick Macmillan
Born: 2nd September 1812
Died: 26th Janruary 1878
The alleged construction of Kirkpatrick's
bicycle was said to be a frame made of
wood, iron-rimmed wood wheels,
handlebars and pedals.

TOM MEIGHAN (FRONTMAN OF THE BAND KASABIAN, AND SCI-FI FANATIC) BOUGHT ELLIOT'S BMX BIKE WHICH FEATURES IN STEVEN SPIELBERG'S CLASSIC FILM E.T FOR £10,000. HE ALSO BOUGHT A LIFE-SIZE MODEL OF E.T AND SPENDS TIME RIDING THE BIKE AROUND HIS FLAT.

E.T. turned a relatively unknown bike brand from Osaka, Japan into a household name overnight. After the movie was released, thousands of retailers were suddenly ordering the Model 3003 that Elliott rides in the movie. The company still makes an anniversary edition you can buy.

THE TERM "ON YOUR BIKE" ORIGINATED IN WALES IN THE 19TH CENTURY AND WAS MOST COMMONLY USED TO WARN AWAY YOUNG MEN WHO WERE INTERESTED IN COURTING A LADY.

There are many other bike related phrases, such as:

"Like riding a bike" – A skill that is easy and memorable.

"The village bicycle" – A promiscuous woman.

"A bumpy ride" – Going into difficulty.

"A woman needs a man like a fish needs a bicycle." – Fish don't need bicycles...

DURING THE TOUR DE FRANCE EVENT, IT IS CONSIDERED POOR FORM IF YOU OVERTAKE THE LEADER WHILE THEY HAVE STOPPE FOR A TOILET BREAK. HOWEVER, TOILET BREAKS AREN'T AS OFTEN AS YOU WOULD IMAGINE, WITH PARTICIPATING CYCLISTS SWEATING ENOUGH TO FLUSH A TOILET 39 TIMES OVER THE COURSE OF THE ROUTE!

There are over 42,000 water bottles used by teams in modern tours. A Guinness World Record was awarded for the largest mosaic print made entirely from recycled materials. This giant mosaic featured the faces of previous Tour De France winners, and aimed to raise awareness for the importance of recycling.

BETWEEN 12,000 AND 15,000 BIKE ARE PULLED OUT FROM THE BOTTOM OF AMSTERDAM'S CANALS EVERY YEAR!

Collectively, Amsterdammers cycle approximately 2 million km each day!

A Trek Madone (also known as the 'Butterfly Bike') is a bicycle designed by artist Damien Hirst. Considered a rare and valuable piece of art, the Butterfly Bike was auctioned for $500,000.

The world's most expensive bike was created by the company House of Gold.

The mountain bike is made from 24K gold and is valued at roughly $1 million.